W9-ACP-093

## WEAPONS OF WAR

# WEAPONS OF THE
# REVOLUTIONARY WAR

## by Matt Doeden

Reading Consultant:
Barbara J. Fox
Reading Specialist
North Carolina State University

Content Consultant:
John C. Hendrickson
Adjunct History Professor
Minnesota State University, Mankato

Capstone
press

Mankato, Minnesota

Blazers is published by Capstone Press,
151 Good Counsel Drive, P.O. Box 669, Mankato, Minnesota 56002.
www.capstonepress.com

*Library of Congress Cataloging-in-Publication Data*
Doeden, Matt.
    Weapons of the Revolutionary War / by Matt Doeden.
    p. cm. — (Blazers. Weapons of war)
    Includes bibliographical references and index.
    Summary: "Describes the weapons used in battles during the Revolutionary
War, including firearms carried by infantry soldiers and artillery weapons" —
Provided by publisher.
    ISBN-13: 978-1-4296-1970-7 (hardcover)
    ISBN-10: 1-4296-1970-8 (hardcover)
    1. United States. Continental Army — Equipment and supplies — Juvenile
literature. 2. Military weapons — United States — History —18th century —
Juvenile literature. 3. United States — History — Revolution, 1775-1783 —
Juvenile literature. I. Title. II. Series.
UF523.D64 2009
623.40941'09033 — dc22                                          2008001992

**Editorial Credits**

Carrie A. Braulick, editor; Alison Thiele, set designer;
    Kyle Grenz, production designer; Jo Miller, photo researcher

**Photo Credits**

Alamy/Mark Summerfield, 29; Alamy/North Wind Picture Archives, 9 (top), 11
(bottom), 12, 17 (bayonets), 22; Art Resource, N.Y., 5; Corbis/Photo Images/
Lee Snider, 19 (top); Courtesy of Independence Seaport Museum, Philadelphia,
28; Getty Images Inc./Stockbyte/George Doyle, cover (top); The Granger
Collection, New York, 13, 14, 17 (tomahawk); The Image Works/The Board
of Trustees of the Armouries/Heritage-Images, 8–9 (bottom), 16 (musket);
The Image Works/National Trust Photographic Library/David Levenson, 23
(cannonballs); James P. Rowan, 15, 17 (pistol), 19 (bottom), 20, 21, 23 (British
mortar, cannon, grapeshot, howitzer), 25, 26–27; Shutterstock/Andreas Meyer,
cover (bottom); Shutterstock/Marilyn Volan (grunge background elements), all;
SuperStock, Inc., 6; www.historicalimagebank.com, 10–11 (top), 16 (musket
shot, rifle, rifle shot), 17 (cavalry sword, rifleman's knife, spontoon head), 23
(howitzer shell)

1  2  3  4  5  6  13  12  11  10  09  08

# TABLE OF CONTENTS

# LET THE BATTLE BEGIN!

Left, right, left, right. Lines of British soldiers march in step. American **colonists** face them. Bang! A gunshot rings out. The battle begins.

**colonist** — a person living in an area that is ruled by another country; Great Britain had colonists living in North America in the 1700s.

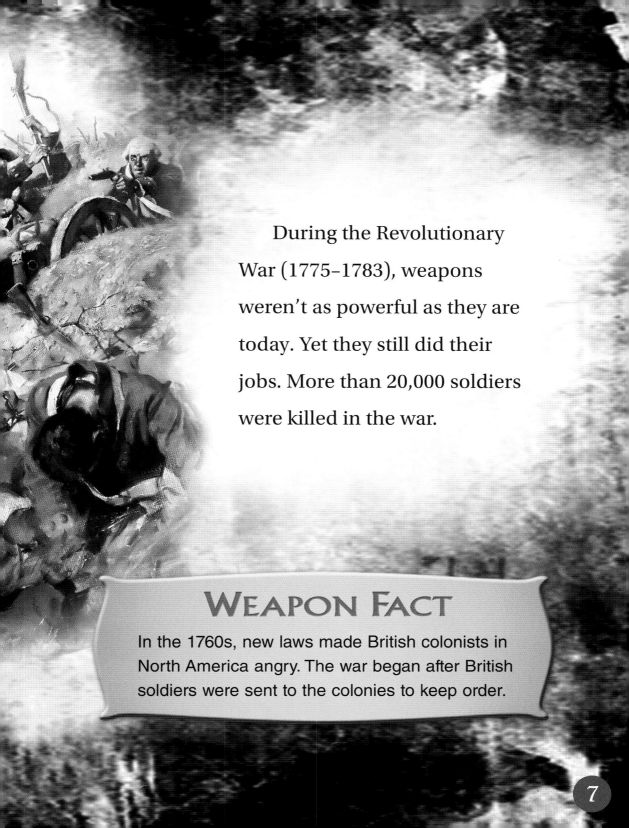

During the Revolutionary War (1775–1783), weapons weren't as powerful as they are today. Yet they still did their jobs. More than 20,000 soldiers were killed in the war.

## WEAPON FACT

In the 1760s, new laws made British colonists in North America angry. The war began after British soldiers were sent to the colonies to keep order.

# PERSONAL WEAPONS

Long guns called muskets fired large lead balls, or shot. But muskets weren't **accurate**. They usually missed targets farther away than 200 feet (61 meters).

> **accurate** — able to hit the target at which a soldier aimed

musket

## WEAPON FACT

Foot soldiers stood side by side and faced their enemies. This way, at least some musket balls would hit their targets.

rifle

Rifles had barrels that made the shot spin. Spinning shot made rifles more accurate than muskets. It also helped rifles hit distant targets. But rifles took longer to load than muskets.

## WEAPON FACT

Colonists sometimes hid in the woods. They fired rifles at the British as they passed by.

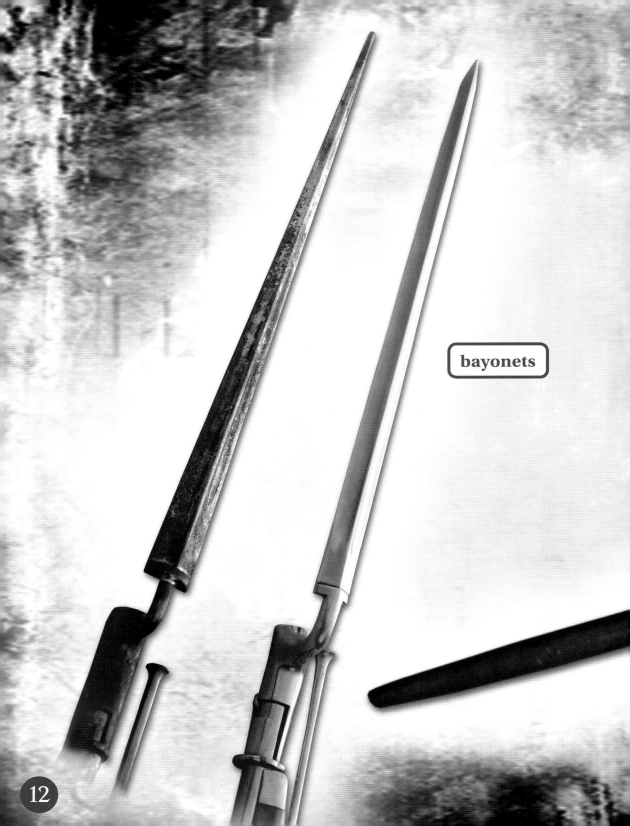

bayonets

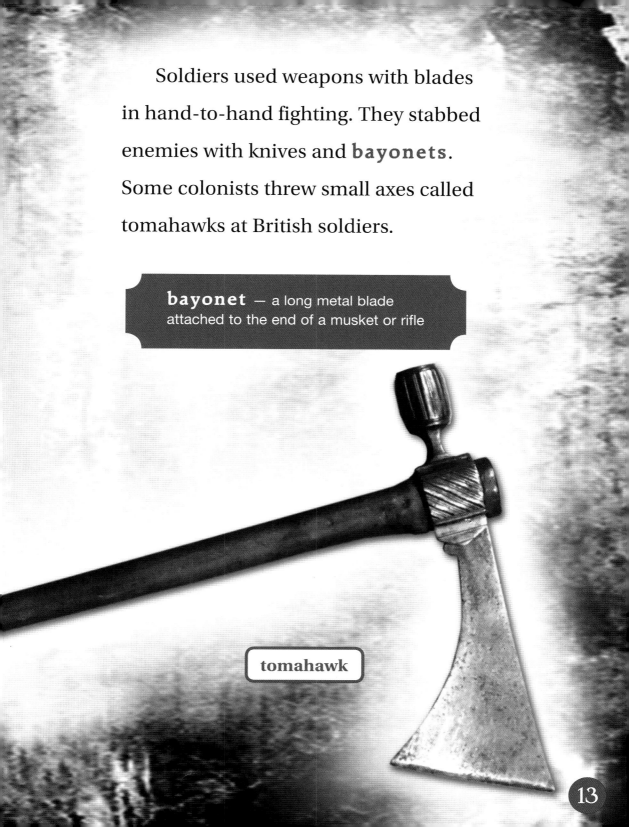

Soldiers used weapons with blades in hand-to-hand fighting. They stabbed enemies with knives and **bayonets**. Some colonists threw small axes called tomahawks at British soldiers.

**bayonet** — a long metal blade attached to the end of a musket or rifle

tomahawk

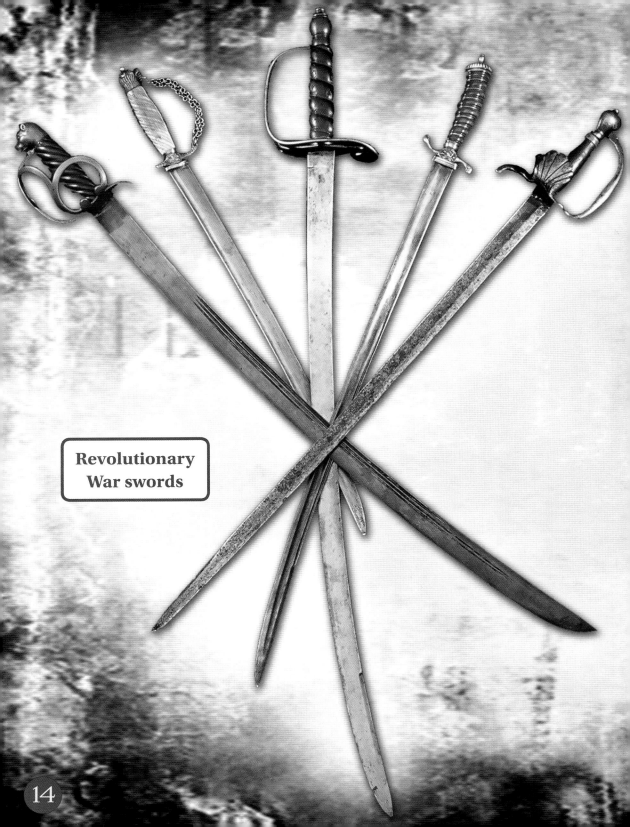

Revolutionary
War swords

14

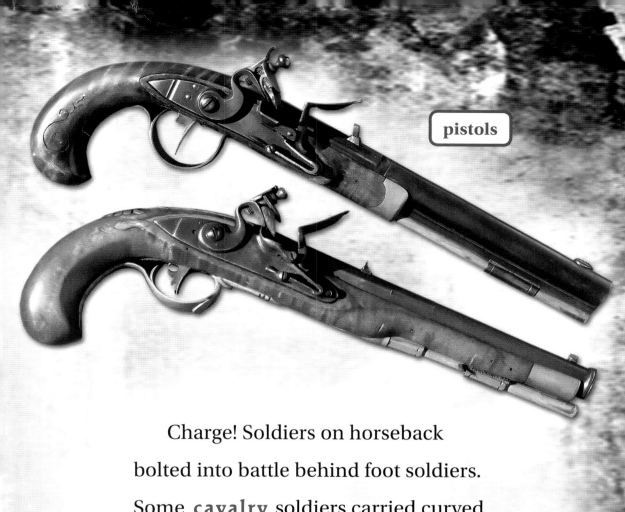

pistols

Charge! Soldiers on horseback
bolted into battle behind foot soldiers.
Some **cavalry** soldiers carried curved
swords. Others fired **pistols**.

**cavalry** — members of an army
mounted on horseback

**pistol** — a small handheld gun

# PERSONAL WEAPONS AND AMMUNITION

musket

musket shot

rifle shot

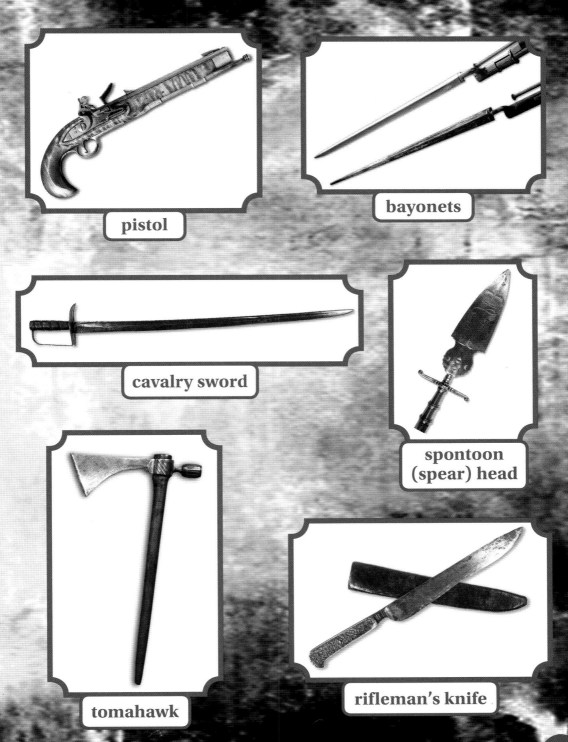

pistol

bayonets

cavalry sword

spontoon
(spear) head

tomahawk

rifleman's knife

17

# ARTILLERY

Artillery packed a powerful punch. The clap of cannon fire rang out across battlefields. A solid 3-pound (1.4-kilogram) cannonball traveled more than 800 feet (244 meters).

artillery — large, powerful guns that are usually mounted on wheels or another supporting structure

cannon

## WEAPON FACT

Cannons also pounded foot soldiers with clusters of small balls called grapeshot.

**12-pound howitzer**

British mortar

Howitzers destroyed targets and sent foot soldiers scrambling. These large cannons fired **shells** high into the air. Mortars worked like howitzers, but they usually fired smaller shells.

**shell** — a small weapon that blows up after hitting its target

In 1778, France joined the American
colonists against the British. French and
British ships then fought fierce battles at sea.

# ARTILLERY AND AMMUNITION

cannon

cannonballs

howitzer

grapeshot

British mortar

howitzer shell

# DEFENSES

Soldiers took shelter when they could. Forts offered some protection. High walls and ditches often surrounded these military stations.

## WEAPON FACT

The British controlled Fort Niagara during the Revolutionary War. This fort was located near the Niagara River in New York.

Fort Niagara
blockhouse

Soldiers fired guns from behind big piles of dirt and mud called earthworks. But earthworks were built only in places where attacks were likely.

## WEAPON FACT

Earthworks with long wooden spikes protected the British fort in Yorktown, Virginia.

Getting supplies to armies was important for both sides. Colonists put logs with pointed iron tips called chevaux-de-frise (shuh-voh-duh-FREEZ) into rivers. The logs blocked British supply ships.

## WEAPON FACT

The singular form of chevaux-de-frise is cheval-de-frise. The word comes from fighters in the Netherlands who used the barriers.

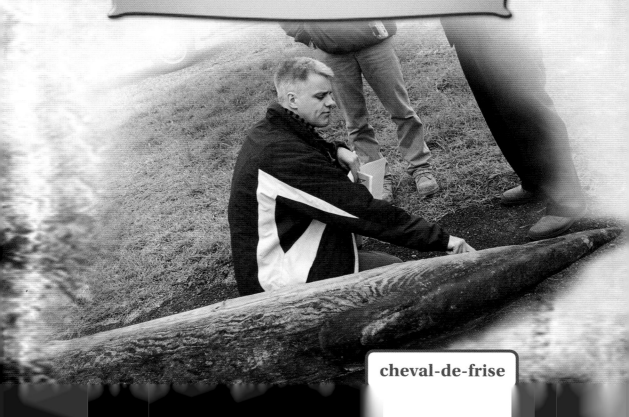

cheval-de-frise

In 1783, the colonists won their freedom from Great Britain. Today, soldiers use more powerful weapons. But you can still find Revolutionary War weapons at military parks and museums.

# GLOSSARY

**accurate** (AK-yuh-ruht) — able to hit the target at which a soldier aimed

**ammunition** (am-yuh-NISH-uhn) — objects that can be fired from guns or cannons

**artillery** (ar-TIL-uh-ree) — large, powerful guns that are usually mounted on wheels or another supporting structure

**barrel** (BA-ruhl) — the long, tube-shaped metal part of a gun through which bullets travel

**bayonet** (BAY-uh-net) — a long metal blade attached to the end of a musket or rifle

**cavalry** (KAV-uhl-ree) — members of an army who fight on horseback

**cheval-de-frise** (shuh-val-duh-FREEZ) — a log with a pointed iron tip placed into rivers to block enemy ships; the plural form is chevaux-de-frise.

**colonist** (KOL-uh-nist) — a person living in an area that is ruled by another country

**pistol** (PIS-tuhl) — a small handheld gun

**shell** (SHEL) — a small weapon that blows up after hitting its target

# Read More

**Anderson, Dale.** *Soldiers and Sailors in the American Revolution.* World Almanac Library of the American Revolution. Milwaukee: World Almanac Library, 2006.

**Hall, Margaret C.** *The History and Activities of the Revolutionary War.* Hands-on American History. Chicago: Heinemann, 2006.

**Parks, Peggy J.** *Weapons.* Yesterday and Today. San Diego: Blackbirch Press, 2005.

# Internet Sites

FactHound offers a safe, fun way to find Internet sites related to this book. All of the sites on FactHound have been researched by our staff.

Here's how:
1. Visit *www.facthound.com*
2. Choose your grade level.
3. Type in this book ID **1429619708** for age-appropriate sites. You may also browse subjects by clicking on letters, or by clicking on pictures and words.
4. Click on the **Fetch It** button.

**FactHound will fetch the best sites for you!**

# INDEX